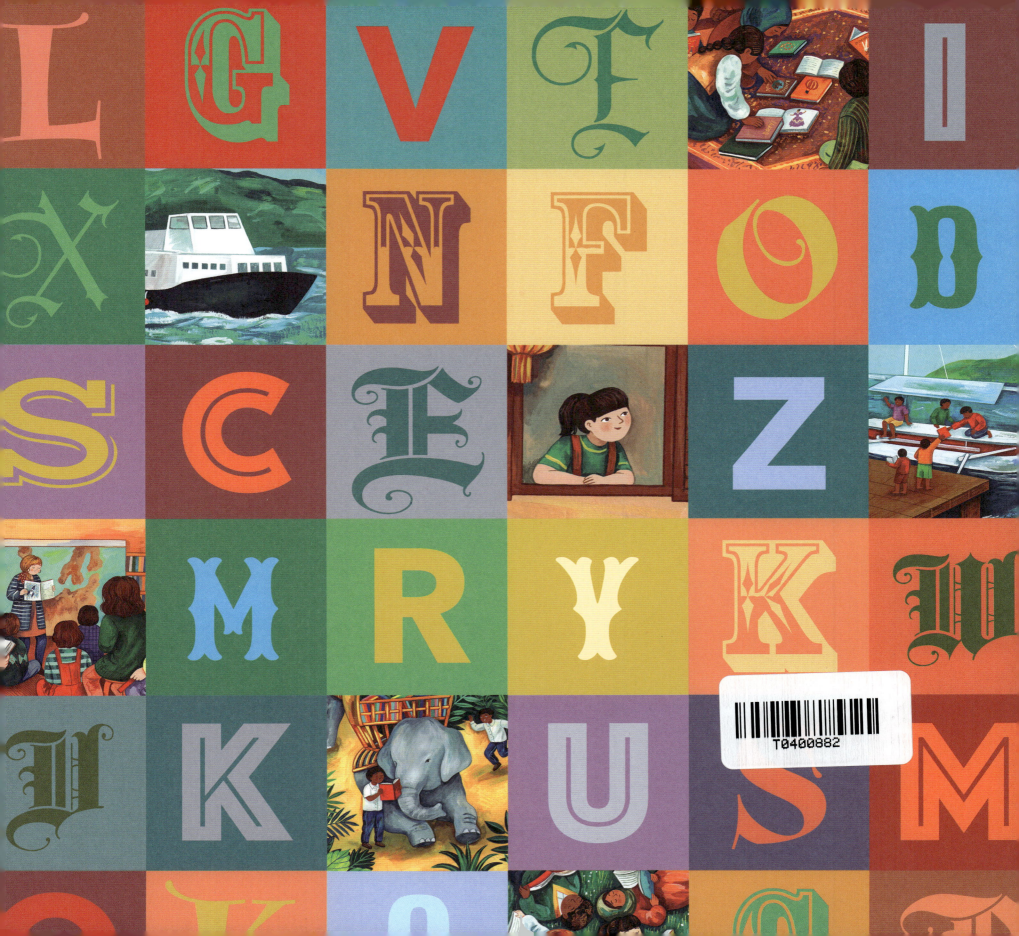

BOOKS
TRAVEL *the* WORLD

For all librarians:

Thank you . . .
For art and skits and songs.
For puppets, poems, and parades.
For book talks, whispering, and inspiring.
For reading parties, buddy reading, and author visits.

Thank you . . .
For asking me to read to you.
For helping me find just the right book.
For a special book you handed me
because you remembered what I liked to read. —J. S.

Text copyright © 2025 by Joan Schoettler

Illustrations copyright © 2025 by Helena Pérez García

Published by Bushel & Peck Books, a family-run publishing house in Fresno, California, who believes in uplifting children with the highest standards of art, music, literature, and ideas. For every book we sell, we donate one to a child in need—book for book. To nominate a school or organization to receive free books, or to find inspiring books and gifts, please visit www.bushelandpeckbooks.com.

All rights reserved. No part of this publication may be reproduced without written permission from the publisher.

Type set in Temeraire and Bookeyed Jack.

LCCN: 2024930653

ISBN: 978-1-63819-186-5

First Edition

Printed in China

1 3 5 7 9 10 8 6 4 2

BOOKS
TRAVEL *the* WORLD

Written by
Joan Schoettler

Illustrated by
Helena Pérez García

*A*ll around the world,
children wait for books.

So . . .

Book lovers cross seas.
They trek up narrow trails,
down steep, rocky paths,
over swift rivers,
and through dark forests.
They journey by foot,
on sturdy animals,
and with unique vehicles,
delivering books to children.

Clomp, clomp!

In Colombia,
a librarian and his donkeys,
Alfa and Beto,
begin their daylong journey.
Packsaddles swell with books
for children in faraway towns.
The teacher reads,
and children do too.
They dream of what they might be.
Astronauts.
Inventors.
Actors.
Before they choose a book for home,
always they say,
"One more story, please!"

Nuz, nuz.

In Kenya at sunrise,
a camel bookmobile
carries books to the nomads,
who move from place to place.
Camels grunt their way across the sand,
and when they come near,
children cheer.

The librarian and children
act out a story.
On straw mats,
young Kenyans explore
tree houses,
snowflakes,
and the ways grandmothers love.

Children return a book
and choose another one.
Librarians pack
and tie boxes to camels
for their next stop,
while children beg,
"One more story, please!"

In Zimbabwe,
four strong donkeys pull
the Library Cart.
Cupboard doors open,
and stories spill out.
Through the pages of books,
children hike mountains,
discover treasures,
or sail the sea.
At the end of the day,
stories become plays,
and children chant,
"One more story, please!"

Ding-a-ling, ding-a-ling!

In France,
the Bibliambule parks.
Canopies shade.
Colorful hammocks unfurl.
Books invite adventures.
"Listen to this!"
Children discover
a walk in the forest,
musical instruments,
and outer space.
Cheerful and thankful for books,
children call out,
"One more story, please!"

Honk, honk!

In the Netherlands,
students clap
as the BeibBus inches closer
and parks near their school.
They cheer when a reused shipping container
slides upward over a fixed, smaller vessel.
Children choose books,
then scramble up to the reading room above.

Librarians share books about
life in faraway places,
the largest trees on earth,
and the perfect nest.
Children listen, learn, and share.
Everyone reads.
Before the bus departs,
children plead, "One more story, please!"

Toot, toot!

In Western Norway,
children scan the waves
for their Library Boat.
Sometimes a film or a show
or an author amuses them,
but books are what they crave!
The librarian sings a story refrain,
inviting children to join.
They discover stories about siblings and friends,
try out new magic tricks,
and study spiders and snakes.
They read, learn, and cry out,
"One more story, please!"

Tsss, tsss!

In Syria,
the brightly painted
Mobile Library
travels through farmland.
At a mosque,
children choose books
displayed on colorful carpets.
They read about
welcoming a new sister,
concerts in a park,
and underwater sea photographers.
Children whisper, "One more story, please!"

In China,
Shared Lady Beetle,
built from an abandoned bike
and filled with books,
lands near a market.
Strong wings unfold.
Shelves of books appear!

In groups or pairs or all alone,
kids read stories about
brave pirates and princesses,
a fisherman and a whale,
and artists and scientists.
Before the librarian
buzzes down the street,
they ask for "One more story, please!"

Clang, clang!

In remote cities in Northern Thailand, children hear the chiming bells of an elephant mobile library. "Hurry, they're coming," kids call together. A librarian rides the elephant and hands books to children. Young readers hear stories of bears, the color blue, and life along the river. Children all agree, "One more story, please!"

Splash, splash!

On a tiny island in Western Indonesia,
children rush to the book boat.
Plastic mats roll out.
Busy hands search for books.
Children sink into pages
on the warm sandy beach.

They imagine,
pretend,
and wonder what they might be
when they grow up.
Like storytellers and actors,
they perform scenes from books.

Sometimes with a stick or finger,
they tell the story in the sand.
Children sing,
"One more story, please!"

Ring, ring!

When Spoke & Word stops
in San Fransisco,
horns sound and pinwheels whirl.
Children delight in reading about
dinosaurs,
math and measuring,
and the moon and stars.
Excited, they sign up
for their very own library card.
When story time ends,
they always request,
"One more story, please."

Tired after their long day,
librarians put up their feet.
And all around the world,
across open seas,
under a setting sun,
in dark forests,
across long bridges,
down hills, and up valleys . . .

children read.

Oh, the Places Librarians Go!

HOW BOOKS TRAVEL THE WORLD

Determined librarians throughout the world go to great lengths to bring books to children. Some travel only in summer, others throughout the year. To deliver books to rural, urban, or remote places, librarians find creative ways to transport the books. They know that literacy improves the future of everyone!

COLOMBIA

When Luis Soriano taught school in northern Colombia, he noticed that his students did not have books available at home to help them progress in their studies. He began carrying armloads of books to their homes, but the distance between houses was great. Soriano started a biblioburro, a mobile library powered by his donkeys, Alfa and Beto. Each donkey can carry 150 books in specially designed saddlebags. Over the years, Soriano added employees and built a brick-and-mortar library in his hometown.

KENYA

The children are excited and happy when they see the camels in the distance. They wait expectantly for the camel bookmobile to come every two weeks. In sweltering heat, librarians and camel drivers travel two or three hours to reach the children. One camel can carry two boxes of 200 books. The other camels carry a tent and supplies.

ZIMBABWE

To provide books in remote areas of Zimbabwe, Dr. Obadiah Moyo designed the world's first donkey-powered mobile libraries. They include shelves for books, lockable compartments for a computer, and space for three rider-drivers. Equipped with solar panels, the mobile carts serve as multimedia libraries, providing internet access, charging phones, and powering a computer.

FRANCE

What is a Bibliambule? It's a hammock-equipped bookmobile scooter filled with children's books ready for summer reading. Seven comfy hammocks invite young readers to find a good book, take the time to enjoy a new story, and develop the habit of reading. The Bibliambule brings books into public spaces for people unable to go to traditional libraries.

NETHERLANDS

The BiebBus is an expanding mobile library especially suited for the narrow streets of the small villages in the Zaan region of the Netherlands. Built with standard 12-meter shipping containers, the library vertically expands to a glass-floored reading room. Designed for children aged 4 to 12, the space invites them to explore, read books, and engage with technology. Parking near primary schools, the BiebBus remains for the whole day. An entire class of children fits into the bus. The three BiebBussen visit locations on a monthly basis, servicing thousands of schoolchildren each year.

NORWAY

Many remote communities along the fjords in Western Norway are too small for local libraries. The solution to providing books for children came in the form of a floating library aboard a ship called *Epos*. Currently, the boat serves as a center for literary events and a traveling bookstore. *Epos* features live entertainment focused on literature like plays, music, author talks, and storytelling. For many young children, this is often their first experience with live events.

SYRIA

In rural areas of Syria's Idlib and Aleppo Provinces, the mobile library visits schools, mosques, and other public places to provide books for children. This service encourages reading in areas where schools have been closed because of war. A dedicated seven-person team reaches out to about 4,000 children.

CHINA

The Shared Lady Beetle is designed as a sleek micro-library on wheels. Abandoned bikes and industrial waste are transformed into a tricycle with a special compartment that serves as a traveling library. Children gather wherever it stops—by schools, in parks, and in public places. Mimicking the way lady-bugs open and close their wings, the compartment reveals shelves filled with books. Children eagerly delve into the world of books and read by the lady beetle's wings.

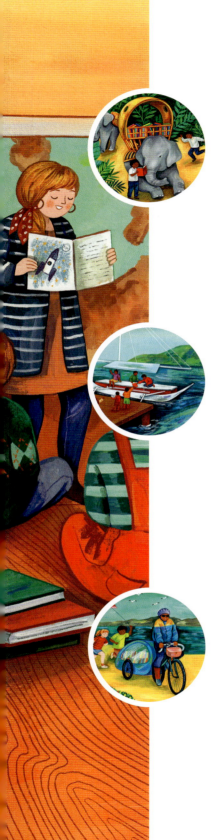

THAILAND

Forty-six villages in remote areas of Northern Thailand benefit from elephant mobile libraries. Children line up on school grounds and welcome the elephants and their two-person teams. Each elephant carries books for the children. The visits are filled with songs, games, and storytelling. The teams focus on elephant conservation, too. Children learn to read and write on metal slates. In 2002, the elephant mobile libraries project was awarded the UNESCO International Literacy Prize.

INDONESIA

Muhammad Ridwan Alimuddin, a journalist in Western Indonesia, combines his love of books and boats and began a book boat mobile library on a *baggo*, a small traditional sailboat. The library boat travels with him and his three-person crew to tiny islands and remote fishing villages. Once on the beaches, plastic mats are unrolled and covered with books. The hum of voices reading fills the air. To travel overland, Alimuddin uses a motorbike, rickshaw, and ATV, and a bamboo raft for crossing rivers. Donations keep his library growing.

UNITED STATES

Spoke & Word is San Francisco Public Library's bike that pulls a trailer filled with books. The peddle-powered library provides a Wi-Fi hotspot, and children can apply for library cards. A rainbow umbrella, three bells, and a loud horn let children know it is nearby. Eager children get to borrow a book to bring home.

 For more information about books around the world, please visit joanschoettler.com

A Colombia
B Kenya
C Zimbabwe
D France
E Netherlands
F Norway
G Syria
H China
I Thailand
J Indonesia
K United States

READING ACTIVITIES

- Tell someone about a book you just read.
- Draw your favorite part of the story.
- Act out a scene from the story.
- Write in your journal about the book.
- Read a book aloud to your friend.
- Share your newly discovered book.
- Share your all-time favorite book.
- Create a mural.
- Invite someone to go to the library with you.

AUTHOR'S NOTE

When I was a child, books were my friends, my inspiration, and my way to explore the world. My interest in children's literature grew as I shared my love of books with young readers and later taught children's literature and storytelling at California State University, Fresno.

I once read about a camel in Kenya delivering books to children, and it sparked my curiosity. I began researching other mobile libraries and found a book boat, an elephant library, and a biblioburro. Determined librarians and teachers create bookmobiles, using imagination, generosity, and persistence to deliver books to children in different areas around the world.

Something very special takes place when a child, a librarian, and a book interact. The librarian invites the listener into the wonderful world of children's literature. Thank you to all the people across our planet who dedicate themselves to placing books in the hands of young readers, making the world a better place. And thank you to my family for your support of my writing.

—J. S.

ABOUT THE AUTHOR

Joan Schoettler's writing demonstrates a global view as her stories traverse the world. Her focus of interest is inspired by true people, intriguing actual events, and the lived experiences of people from diverse backgrounds. *The Honey Jar: An Armenian's Escape to Freedom*, her first middle-grade novel, received the California Book Award, Juvenile, Gold Medal Book 2024. Joan's other picture books include *Ruth Asawa: A Sculpting Life*, *A Home for George*, and *Good Fortune in a Wrapping Cloth*. Joan earned a master of arts degree in reading and language from Fresno Pacific University. She taught children's literature and storytelling at California State University, Fresno. Joan lives with her husband in California where they raised three sons. Her grandchildren continue to inspire her writing. Visit her at joanschoettler.com.

ABOUT THE ILLUSTRATOR

Helena Pérez García is a Spanish illustrator whose work has appeared across magazines, newspapers, packaging, and books for children and adults internationally. Helena's primary medium is gouache, and her main sources of inspiration are art, literature, and cinema. Some of her clients include Penguin Random House, The Body Shop, Tate Publishing, *The Financial Times*, *Reader's Digest*, and *Corriere della Sera*, among many others.